Journey to Embarkation

A Reflection in Poetry

Bob Ambrose, Jr

Parson's Porch Books

Journey to Embarkation – A Reflection in Poetry
ISBN: Softcover 978-1-951472-25-2
Copyright © 2016 by Robert B. Ambrose, Jr.

Revised edition, 2024

All rights reserved. No part of this book may be reproduced or transmitted in any form or by any means, electronic or mechanical, including photocopying, recording, or by any information storage and retrieval system, without permission in writing from the publisher.

The cover photograph and the photograph of the author on the back cover were by David Noah, Winterville, Georgia.

To order additional copies of this book, contact:

Parson's Porch Books
1-423-475-7308
www.parsonsporch.com

Parson's Porch Books is an imprint of Parson's Porch & Company (PP&C) in Cleveland, Tennessee. PP&C is an innovative company which raises money by publishing books of noted authors, representing all genres. All donations from contributors and profits from publishing are shared with the poor.

With gratitude
for the memory of my parents
and the presence of my siblings, wife, and daughter:

    Robert Brown Ambrose
    Ruth Gilmore Ambrose

    Sandra Ambrose Smith
    Richard Forrest Ambrose
    Ronald James Ambrose

    Kathryn June Hatcher
    Sarah Kathryn Ambrose

Table of Contents

Prelude

The Comfort of Fading	8

Farewell to Summer

The View from Grandma's Kitchen	12
Summer Lakeside Grace	14
The Sense of Cicada	16
To Mothers Watching Offspring Part	17
Telemachus Tends His Driveway	18
Lines Composed a Few Miles Out of My Head While Fleeing an Unpacked Garage During Fall Cleaning	20
A Farewell to Summer	22
Old Riverside Oak	24
A Summer Morning's Leave	26
To Our Children Leaving Home	29
To My Two-Year-Old Daughter, A Quarter Century Later	32
The Memory of a Summer Postcard	34
Cathedral Dreams in Salt and Sand	36
An Elegy for Aralee Strange	39

To Cross The Northern Tier

The Mountain West	42
The Great Plains	44
The Lake Country	46
The Great Lakes	48
The Appalachians East	50

Journey to Embarkation

A Way in The Wilderness	54
To The End of Haight	56
Inner Sunset, Morning Rain	58
Ladies of The Lake	59

A Sunday Afternoon Island Dream	60
A Friday Morning Devotional in Iglesia Evangelica Metodista	62
Jessica's Blessing	64
The Night Music of San Rafael De Guatuso	66
The Girl's Guava Tree	68
Waiting for Advent in Istanbul	69
Egyptian Sunrise	70
The Diminutive of Grace	73
Yangtze Blues	76
Last November Sunset	79
To Go to Patagonia	80
Afternoon Joe	82
Watching After August Rains	84
From The Deck of the New Horizons	86
Light Bodies	88
Lessons for The Fallen	90
The Second Soul of November	91
Journey to Embarkation	94

Postlude

A Remembrance of Terminals Past	98
Acknowledgments	101

Prelude

The Comfort of Fading

There were years of prime
when I looked upon a living bay
pulsing with life, pulled
by celestial bodies, and saw

numerical mesh
stretching through
the sterile ether.
Such a stately parade

of symbols set in spare beauty –
partial c's sliding slopes
of Q and E, of x and t,
but no longer.

The crystalline equations fade;
their symbols spill
off dog-eared pages
graced with arcs of coffee stain

in manuals with my name inside
and broken backs, now boxed
and stored in cardboard tombs
of moth and mildew, must and tears.

I find my life now softly fallen
in the gentle in-between

while plowing through uncharted now
as Voyager past the heliopause

no longer here
but not yet there.

So I shut my eyes in warm sun
and drift down whole days.

The world is my back yard,
the afterlife unfenced.

I wander a peaceable kingdom
where voices chant in strange tongues

from the distance of dreams,
and though I cannot catch their meaning,

sure as Voyager shoots beyond,
I shall sing their soul, unknowing.

Farewell to Summer

The View from Grandma's Kitchen

Day after faithful day
Grandmother Gilmore rose before dawn
in a tiny log home, carved into Carolina woods.
Grandpa sleeps

as she tiptoes to
her snug kitchen, warm as a womb
standing by the iron-stained sink
looking out

on a weathered well-house
hard by the side yard oak
hemmed in by hickory
flanked by the forest

in darkness beyond.
Night softens, coffee perks and oats congeal
as she stirs and hums her Gospel songs –
Maxwell House

Quaker Oats
and Precious Lord would see her through.
Did she dream of their life in the city again?
She lived high on the hog

for a Hickerson girl
till God laughed and times turned –
the good life got away again.
With Peace in the Valley

the black night recedes
through shadows and gray
to one more day much like the last.
The mama cat

would be hungry again
so she scrapes a plate of table scraps
to place beside the back porch step
with a dish of milk

for the kittens to lap.
She butters another pan biscuit
for the faraway grandchild hovering
by the kitchen table

carried aloft
on comic book dreams. She pours his juice
in a jelly jar as he bides his time
to warmth of day

to find his own way
through the woods and the fields
through the toils and the snares
till he no longer hears

her own voice in his mind.
But memory bears her blessed assurance
from over the Jordan in Beulah Land.
So I rise in the darkness

a half century on, still humming
her early morning song, still dreaming
my way through the vastness beyond
but perking and stirring a day like the last.

Summer Lakeside Grace
In dreams of yesterday – from boyhood in north Florida

There were high summer Sundays
so blessed, instead of church
we'd head for Starke.

Unshackled from Seersucker,
kicking off shoes
for swim suits and flip flops

and freedom to breathe,
we packed the family wagon
squirming in the back seat.

While Mom passed out peppermint,
Dad steered us south
to ski the day at Kingsley Lake.

Four brown and freckled
stair step children carve
the crystal surface to exhaustion

then snorkel the shallows
floating a dreamscape
like airships over fairy towns

with towers of algae and silverside
minnows by forests of lake grass
and plains of fine sand.

Perfect days wane
as we ride home with Ray Charles
crackling on the car radio –

Sing the song, children.
A half century softens
when his chorus confirms

I can't stop loving you
and I live again in memory
of a lonesome time

sensing the shadow
of an awful obligation –
growing up means going on.

Halfway home we stop once more
by the random roadside stand
to choose a ripe melon

forged of water and sun
much like our happy lives,
for even now I close my eyes

and taste it yet –
the sweetness of late youth,
yielding.

The Sense of Cicada

When morning chill
   subsides to day
      soft air will trill
   to waves of cicada
in rhythmic insistence

that pulse the summer
   with resonant tides
      piercing the decades
   to float an old spirit
outside of its time.

Soft evening shadows
   hold an old homestead
      with cabin and garden
   once carved from the forest
by grandfather's hand.

Out back in the darkness
   young parents and uncles
      with aunties and elders
   are weaving old stories
conversing again.

Eternity beckons
   as voices are merging
      with swells of a chorus
   from forests departed
and family dispersed.

Perhaps we shall sing
   with the sense of cicada
      that time is illusion
   the earth is our nursery
and summer abides.

To Mothers Watching Offspring Part

It was the church bells
from just past Five Points
as late afternoons lingered
on the cusp of evening, ringing
family home in those happy years

Till one by one we left.

But ah, to rise to distant cause,
discover wings of light and gauze
like tiny Monarchs born to fall
who feel the ache of far away,
forsake the fields of yesterday

To take the wind and open skies.

It is an odd quintessence —
the noble hyperbole, glorious lies
and naïve dreams of youthful tribes
that glide above beleaguered lives
of mothers watching offspring part

As bells toll love and ancient loss.

What comes of cocoons came
over her heart as dusk by dark
the shadows crept to Gospel
chimes and childhood rhymes,
the sweet debris of golden times

In mommy's world now left behind.

Telemachus Tends His Driveway
Thoughts revisiting Tennyson's Ulysses and his son, Telemachus

The world shimmers
beyond the kaleidoscopic canopy
decorating my driveway
with layers of leaves.

So I set my purpose
    make a plan
    grasp the rake
    execute the task
mindfully, at first
while two tired dogs
watch, curiously
indifferent to achievement,
snouts down the driveway,
waiting for their goddess
to drive home.

And I too wait
as something in my soul
watches with practiced patience
its own wild yearning
to pursue that grey spirit
through archways to unknown worlds
    and yet

I have lived so far
in the common sphere
with Telemachus, tied
to due adoration of gods
both false and true, balancing
dutiful with discerning
over slow, prudent decades:
    of discipline
    of accomplishment
    of exiting gracefully
a life, not unhappy

    while a soul that could soar
kept safely to ground.

Can Telemachus, retired
capture Ulysses' soul?
Can a good son
    sail lightly
        beyond the sunset
    on a warm autumn breeze
        and swirl of dry leaves?

My solace is a still vision
of grey Telemachus
    transcending duty
grasping his own salvation
    in the next task,
        and the next
pursued with a passionate
    kindness.

Lines Composed a Few Miles Out of my Head while Fleeing an Unpacked Garage During Fall Cleaning

Worse than wandering through Walmart
in search of the elusive item
the one true token
amidst a thousand false idols
assaulting my psyche
in aisle forty-two.

Harder than hosting a preteen soiree
in a darkened rollerdrome
where disco strobes sweep dingy floors
and racks of speakers blast strange tunes
to squeals of young she-sirens
circling their dreams.

You've been there too, I trust –
the tightrope frays
and you're hanging by a torn nerve;
the coherence engine quits
and you're stranded on the shoulder
with a thousand-yard stare;

Your garage devolves
to Augean stables
and you, sir, no Hercules
as you stand, slump-shouldered
sweat strewn to entropy
amid the ruins of one less day.

I have wandered confused in the Khan el-Khalili
washed in the call of merchant and muezzin
lost in the heart of the Grand Bazaar
through interior alleys of Istanbul
down halls of rug and spice
by all the bling you'll never need.

And I've raced through the bowels of MIT
searching for a shifted course,
clock winding down on the final exam.
I do not remember the subject now
but learned her remorseless lesson –
a hard clock marks our mortal time.

So I seek the peace of pilgrimage
in a slow country drive
straight through the senescence of winter
over amber Georgia hills
across the muddy Oconee
to the company of poets

Where the blessed mood comes,
grace to the unworthy
which cannot be corralled
nor bartered, nor brokered,
but sufficient for a day redeemed
as manna to the wandering mind.

A Farewell to Summer
In memory of my mother.

One on each side, my brothers
hoist the folding beach chair
and carry with care
this now frail woman
    across the access

to the edge of the sea
to soak her toes in a tidal caress
to feel the roar
    and the silence
to take that one last look

at the wide spaces she wandered
with childhood dreams
her own, her children's
    her children's children
in those magical margins

where she honed her vocation
spinning lifelines of happiness
to secure young souls
    within her spell
of sunny summer wonder.

Beach grass bends
in the prevailing wind
as they anchor loose sands
to foundations of impermanence
    that shift imperceptibly

through human lives
and even endless summers
must yield their time
to make way for new
    beginnings.

The wind blows which way it will
      we do not know where
or why, and so let go only because
we must, and claim that bitter prize —
our due share of reluctant wisdom.

Her short hair tangles today
with a warm ocean breeze
that mixes sand and salt
and the sweet smell of sunblock.
      She sheds no tears

but sets her countenance
to the infinite horizon
with weary resolve
      to honor what was,
what must be again

and to go her way into autumn
with the grace of summer
clutching lightly to the backs
of tiny boys grown tall
      in the sunshine of her life.

Old Riverside Oak
In memory of my father.

It was early March then,
a year and eternity past,
we brought Dad home.
From his old blue chair,
he peered through new
windows, not his own

as snow blankets froze
our Southern woodland
into hard white silence
and gray flows flooded
the shallow river shoals
with an icy hush.

Do you remember
that dark night's cold
when bitter winds descended
from bleak polar plains
showering limbs and ice
over frozen foundations

of our beleaguered home?
Powerless, huddled
in a house leaking warmth
we covered this fragile,
this gentle-souled man
with blankets and love.

Strong against the night,
but in strength unavailing
over softening banks,
the old riverside oak
surrendered itself to swirling gray
and lodged in downstream shallows.

A year now it's been,
a year of great loss, a year

nurturing growth
    and senescence,
and the canopy fills again
closing gaps with lacy green

    softening the void
now filled with light,
but still, the void.
Springtime truth emerges
    from emptiness
with whispers of hope –

Mortal life, though dust
is forever redeemed
for we function within
    a greater whole
which cannot quite
be resolved

in the fun-house mirrors
of our dim perception.
So we see now
    in part
but miss the unity
beyond

that surrounds the void
    in a cosmic embrace
apprehended, if at all
in a place beyond words
expressed in the silence
that speaks to the heart.

The old oak, which served the sky
still provides structure. On trunk
and limb where hawk pairs nested
mud turtles bask, gleaming
in bright sun
    over fresh spring flow.

A Summer Morning's Leave
July, 9, 2009

1.

Last night I held your body
    frail, light
    limp from effort,

Until, finally, sleep
    blessed comfort, sleep
    deep sleep, deepening still

While I marked each hour of darkness
    counting your breath
    on the back of my hand

And your pulse in my fingertips
    as steady through
    the night

Breath eased, your heart
    held, you still
    here. Still.

2.

Early morning is my time
    when the world turns fresh
    and days open doorways –
    To run the rolling land

Pressing breath against pain
    cresting hills, clearing lungs,
    the good earth passing fast,
    to glide with Gaia,

Slow dancing tai chi in grass
    bare feet stained green
    finding balance
    in fleeting moments

Feeling the free flow of time
    rushing through my veins
    still in the flush of strength, still
    grasping for grace.

3.

In the vigor of youth you
    held my premature
    body gently, firmly
    against death, and
    carried me home.

Steady through the years you
    loved one woman
    well, and with her,
    raised up family
    to love and play.

You lived solid, you
    completed duty
    with discipline,
    softening through
    decades of devotion.

And in the stillness of age,
    dear man, you
    accepted decline
    with dignity,
    and in the letting go
        found grace.

4.

I return to your side
one final time, where
forever now
we stand in sacramental hush
heads down, eyes
averted

in solemn witness, so
still, this world
in which I hold your worn-out body
vainly against death
and feel the final brush
of love in your sandpaper chin, still
warm yet now
against my salty face.

5.

You took your leave this summer morning.

6.

Now, early morning is our time.
    I will carry you in my muscles
    in my wind, in my balance
        in my spirit

Until they, too, fail
    and you, once again,
    carry me
        home.

To Our Children Leaving Home
Reflections on a vision relayed by Susan Richardson

It is always so,
they go forth
bearing our biology
passed on from dawn
of life's first day.
But so much more
they bear our dreams
on loan since Eve
awoke to wonder,
pondered, suffered,
lost her Abel.
Ever to the left
behind who love
enough to let
them go, may God
grant visions, offer
signs.

    Of fair spring skies and foals in fields
    enclosed by fences, sturdy gates
    restraining safe the bounding colt
    and bright-eyed filly. Safe, but kept
    confined too long, they'll never be
    what God designed, and so to grow
    and tame proud hearts, we lead them out
    to wider fields across the hill where
    far-off fences, unmanned gates give room
    to run consumed by joy, constrained
    till strong. The same our young.

But God steals hearts
and leaves gates open,
gates unguarded
but by love, a love
impressed inside
the growing, love
that's fit for wider
fields, a love more

fierce than wildest
demon, love beyond
our gentle vision.

> Within our gates are wide green pastures,
> lush enough to feed a soul, sustaining
> life a while, forever. Open gates, though,
> promise more: they hold back magic,
> mysteries, wild valleys, distant shores
> and shadows, room to roam beyond our
> vision, we who love them desperately.

They will go
through gates in time,
they will pass
beyond protection,
they will wander
far lands guarded
but by love,
and they will find
new fields to savor,
pastures they can call
their own.

> So stay a while, forever with us, safe
> in fences, you who go. You leave behind
> you ones more fragile than you'll ever come
> to know. But go with God and bear great dreams
> beyond the gate if that must be, if that
> is now your destiny. We will await
> your coming home.

Yet all this, naught but
idle thought about the
sacred course of life
from hopes and fears
of aging hearts. We
open wide the inner
gate, remove the reins
and give a pat, then

leaning back we watch
you take short halting
steps. With somewhat
noble toss of mane
your stately stride
turns into trot
then frisky canter;
prancing forth, you
lightly trample
tender trails through
meadow grass, and by
the time we turn
away, you've
disappeared
across the
hill.

    I latch the inner gate, and my heart
    catches, recalling how it felt to prance.
    When you come home, let's plan to dance.
    I'll let you lead. Please take my hand.

To My Two-Year-Old Daughter, a Quarter Century Later
Bear Hollow Children's Zoo, Athens, Georgia

I wandered through Bear Hollow
    with you once again
        bouncing lightly on my shoulder
  sharing fresh Saturday memories
        under blue crystal sky
        and golden yellow sun
    in a time gone by.

You delight today
    in the open possum playscape
        with pale coat female
and her homely prehensile tail,
        licking peanut butter from the perch
        and gently grooming
    her dainty pink nose.
You watch, intent

and I hold your tiny hand
    tight against the decades
        that press, inexorable
    blurring memory,
        softening vivid presence.

        Yet my breath still catches
    when I recall
a quarter century hence
    your wispy blond curls
        framing the face of delight itself
        as you laugh
    and your spirit shines

    through other eyes today –
though differing in hue and homeland,
        they share the same sparkle.

And I am gray presence, passive
    witness to their wonder
        which they will carry
            into unknown worlds
        that you will build together
           from the hopes and embers
we leave behind.

The Memory of a Summer Postcard
Niles Beach, Gloucester, Massachusetts

Somewhere, my friend, now fading,
frayed, what once was bright
in living hues is now pastel
and washed out gray. It seems

much like old memory, this
rocky harbor picture postcard
captured worlds within its borders –
crescent beach and bracing water,

muted light and frozen sparkles,
far-off figures joined to shadows,
silhouettes at rest forever, sifted
from the flowing stream.

An aging man there sat alone
just watching seas; he seemed
to ponder something lost
some time ago – forgotten ways,

abandoned goals, or maybe
supper – silhouettes withhold
their secrets, time sweeps
currents seldom crossed.

Today I walk with niece and nephews, bride
and partners, past old homes with fragrant arbors
to a strip of sand and shadow, smells of salt
and washed up slime, high shrieks aloft

on ocean breezes, sparkles playing over water,
loved ones laughing, lounging, waiting, youthful
vigor bursting through, they yearn for someplace
new to anchor – softer sand lies ever farther.

Y'all go on your own, ya hear.
There's something here I need

to ponder — what that gray man
gazing saw and how it felt

in weathered skin with waning
days and winter coming.
Let me drift off August harbors
let cold currents sweep me free

inhabit realms I'll never see
pursue their ghosts relentlessly,
replenish dreams of those I meet,
refinish postcard memories.

Skedaddle please just leave me be,
your restless spirits must press on.
There's happiness in what I have —
warm sun baking sea from skin

honest hunger, ample supper
family style with playful banter
served to salve the fraying edges
well suffice to staunch the graying.

Catch'ya in the evening chill I say
aloud to no-one near as déjà vu
sweeps ever stronger, overwhelming
memory. With laughter trailing

distantly, they merge into my postcard
harbor, tintype silhouettes to treasure,
relics held by love forever —
living hues shall never fade.

Cathedral Dreams in Salt and Sand

When Gaia dreams of happy times
she makes an August beach again
and recreates our former lives
the swirl of sibling – parent – child
converge once more along the strand
to build a playscape castle-strong
with towers, turrets, moats and walls
well-fortified with broken shells
to hold against onrushing tide
and toddler joy unleashed on sand
quite unconstrained, still unashamed
to taste the foam fresh off the ocean
chasing wavelets back to sea
from splashing edge of tidal line
immersed in rhythms of the deep.

    The sparkling whoosh
        and hissing sigh
a pause and whoosh
        and hiss again
eternity lies
        in sparkle and sigh
in plaintive cries
        that pierce the tide
the shriek of gull
        and wide-eyed child
the wind, the marsh
        the march of time
as oceans ebb
        as oceans flood
the line recedes
        the line returns
embracing our castles
        erected in fun
erasing our idols
        to midsummer sun
reclaiming our castles
        of sparkle and sigh

    as pound and whoosh
        subside through hiss
    to sigh and pause
        and pound again
    till all lies flat
        along the strand
    our traces cleansed
        beneath the sky.

The beach reboots with each new tide
and with each dawn come fresh new signs
the dance of bird and fiddler crab
their stride and scuttle mark short lives
impressed on prints of last night's tide
with curving ripples caught in sand
where mornings saw us start again
to build new castles at the line
where tidal reach exceeds its grasp
and drops new loads of broken lives
from shell-borne burden, structures rise
and laughter thrives amidst the sighs
when daylight fades on childhood lives
small silhouettes cross red-streaked sky
as glowing days give way to night.

    So year by year
        we'd go again
    to Gaian dreamscapes
        salt and sand
    and strings of days
        outside of time
    to build our children
        castle strong
    shaped and formed
        by loving hands
    and fortified
        by strands of sun
    with salt of oceans
        salt of tears

when dreams erode
    like drying sand
when fresh winds rise
    when waves pile high
when time returns
    as bracing tide
it's we who long
    and lag behind
their fortunes rise
    from times gone by
in Gaia's dreams
    where joy thrives
their sun ascends
    to sparkle, sigh
from sand cathedral
    dreams of life.

An Elegy for Aralee Strange
Aralee Strange – Founder, Athens Word of Mouth

In some place primeval
where rhythms take form
your spirit's reborn

as sirens sing a softened call
and chastened furies chant refrain
till Sybil blows a soulful riff

and hears your smoky voice proclaim –

It's just the broken way of things
    that what you love will leave too soon.

Though none could say
what kind of faith sustained
your Timberdance years,

a warm spring bathed your soul,
submerging self to nurture words
in perfect strangers.

Such a poet never dies,
they just transcend.
Their words become an epitaph

their thoughts a meme,
their spirits, muse.
Unburdened of body

returned to the source,
to the place beyond words
where they go to be born,

your essence awaits –

A brief note, held sweet
    against silence
echoes forever
    the memory of grace

To Cross the Northern Tier

In May 2015, Carol Myers retired and set out from Anacortes, Washington on a solo, unsupported bicycle trek across America. She arrived at Orr's Island, Maine on August 22.

The Mountain West
Anacortes, Washington through Logan Pass, Montana

Is it vision, dream, or *deja-vu*?
I'm sipping espresso at Moka Joe's
three miles east of Anacortes, first stop
down a summer road that ends in the cold

Atlantic. I savor the morning shadows
of my next new life. A continent calls.
Its mountain ranges rise before me,
mile-high passes carve the heights,

constraining my path to the Plains.
Washington caps the North Cascades,
Sherman cuts the Kettle Range,
and Logan tops the Rockies.

The charismatic elevations loom.
But more than heights—the hills
and heat, the toils and snares, what
lies between. Unknowns await,

yet I bring what I need. I will move
by my own instinct and keep up
with no one. I will stretch out on rocks
and ponder. I'll pare down

and live each day by the sun.
I will work up a sweaty grime
and bathe in cold lakes. I will go
lightly across the land.

I may feast on fresh eggs
or dine on days-old bags of food,
drink huckleberry shakes
or stanch thirst with stale water.

There will be days dogged by heat
when I arrive in a red daze
coated in a salty sheen and think
how sweet it feels to be alive.

For in the end, not heights nor heat
nor trials between, but what we find
that lies within. Soon I will be gone
from here. We travel alone together.

The Great Plains
Logan Pass, Montana through Fargo, North Dakota

Down, down the long descent
down from the snows of Logan Pass
to land-of-the-wind where the wide
empty opens onto arid steppes
and descendants of nomadic tribes
inhabit the shadow of grandeur.

I sail east on a tailwind and fly
by pastures and pea fields, by sleek
turbines lining dry ridges. I wave
to the west-bound Amtrak and roll
through lonely towns with sad taverns
where food is forlorn afterthought.

From Rudyard to Hingham, from Havre
on, faith is a friendly bar in an alien land;
hope is a bathroom around the next bend.
Perhaps the next pantry has lattes and scones,
beef jerky, cheese bits, and trail gorp to go.
And always I go. Day by day I take the road

through open fields of shifting hues that shimmer
in the morning air, then trudge the miles of muted
tones that anchor the afternoon sky-drama.
I go by the goodness of people and swear
by the kindness of strangers. Angels
wander grocery aisles and blessings

leaven the road. An old man hurries
from his home to offer the grace
of water as I pedal through his
reservation, onto rolling green
ridges, into relentless headwinds
and heat. I hew to the backroads

but hop the shoulder of an empty Interstate
when crumbling asphalt of Highway 10
lodges the treads of my tires. I push
by the oil derricks of Dickinson
and manicured lawns of Taylor
to pause in retreat at Assumption Abbey.

As I tack the shifting winds I dream
of shaded oases with lakes and trees —
Minnesota pulls me on. It pulls me
past tall grain towers and beyond
long trains towing tank cars of oil.
It pulls me through the traffic of Bismarck.

The land greens by degrees and Earth
unveils her sensuous curves. White
daisies line the roadside. Green
hay carpets the horizon. Distant
depressions tucked in ponds are tiny
puddles in the intimate empty.

You cross the plains by persistence,
pedal stroke by pedal stroke, fueled
by a root beer float, lifted by lattes,
pushed by pretzels and Kit-Kat bars,
stoked by fast food bacon burgers.
You cross a continent meal to meal.

Where did the prairie end?
Was it the cafe in Kindred conjuring
the ways of Lake Wobegon?

It was gone by Fargo. I slept
at a HoJo with hot tub and pool

then slipped away into soft morning rain.

The Lake Country
Pelican Rapids, Minnesota to Gladstone, Michigan

There is a land set halfway home,
the sculpture of sunlight and storm,

a rolling canvas molded from prairies
and painted with pastures, copses, and corn.

There's a psalm of abundance sung
by the earth in the voice of wind and rain

on shaded lanes by silver lakes
as summer daylight … wanes.

-

The vale is a place of parting,
where road companions peel away

true to their own imperative. I steer
my bike the northern way, straight

into angst of daily toils, beset
by head winds, heat, and storms.

My roads climb unending swells
closed in by corn row monotony.

Plagues of black flies rise from bogs
and evening mosquitos sequester my tent.

My spirit is mired in the daily must
as midnight morphs into dawn.

-

But surely the wind will shift again,
the hills will flatten, skies shall blue,

and I will sit by still waters. There is rest
on the shores of Big Sand Lake, renewal

birthed in a kindness. This is the quiet
of my trip, when adventure becomes

ordinary and pleasure is taken in maps
and meals, in quenching sips and soaking

baths, in rotating pedals and finding my
pace, easing across the countryside.

-

There is a land set halfway home,
a gentle land — I shall return ...

another day. But now is the time to be
gone. To encounter the empty timberland

as I enter the East outside Escanaba
and camp by the bay of a sweet water sea.

The Great Lakes
Gladstone, Michigan to Port Ontario, New York

From the pine-scented northern shores,
sprinkled with seasonal hunting motels
where AC is an oscillating fan arranged
by a wedged open window;

to an idle day in Saint Ignace
and Main Street on Mackinac Island
immersed in tourists and tidy shops,
clean as a Disney theme-scape;

past Harbor Springs and Charlevoix,
reeling from excessive wealth,
to an evening dip in the shallows at dark
in the peace of Petoskey Park —

I love the big waters of Michigan
with orchards of cherries by
Grand Traverse Bay, but I leave
for the homes of old Huron,

the currents and eddies of River
St. Clair, which carry the freighters
to docks in Detroit and ferries
across into Chatham. I would

loiter once more through my time
in Ontario, idling past the pleasant
farms where shiny windmills slowly
spin an indolent summer breeze.

I'd embrace again the horizons
of Erie, lingering in a beach cafe
to watch an old couple watching
the waves, just passing their days

in the sun. I mark my hours by moving
on, by gray bluffs and hardy flowers
along an unassuming coast, where
weeds secure the shoreline. I glide

the shadows on Erie's expanse as
meditation moves me east, shedding
thoughts with shifting views. The mist
precedes the thunder approaching Niagara

Falls where wonder is wrapped
in a rainbow, reflected in people
the world brings to me. I treasure
this stage of delightful days, each

in peaceful succession, each more
precious as they dwindle. Now I
move through a world of internal
cues and I move at my own deliberate

pace by Rochester up to Selkirk Shore
where I contemplate the evening glow
as purple drains through deepening
hues until at last the darkness soothes

and all is mere external. Now I go
with the peace of the fresh water seas
as my journey turns to interior hills
and hollows of old Appalachia.

The Appalachians East
Port Ontario, New York to Orr's Island, Maine

If heaven resembles the Swift House Inn
as haven for wayfaring bicycle souls,
then I'll savor the dwindling stage

of my life. My final days are preordained,
set on where I'll sleep each night, locked
in to how I will get there:

ride, rest, hydrate, eat,
pedal, shift, pedal, coast,
do it over, again

again

by lakes and mountains, pastures, forest,
field and farm to camps and inns
until at last the epic ...
                                      ends.

Should we speak of scenery?

        How clouds nestle
                the creases
        of mountains.

How dark
green tunnels
wind the interior
of Adirondack Park
to moody lakes
lined with fir,
brooding
in the evening
drizzle.

How the intimate vistas of old Vermont
hold a tangible sweetness filling the air
with August heat and fresh-mown hay.

How the steep
ascent of Kancamagus,
up the slopes to Beaver Lake
unveils another most wonderful view

of my trip. But what of my journey, plunging
through memory and rumination, a summer
of moving meditation? How I passed through

the dreamland of Iroquois Nation carrying
my incarnations inside, from the awkward
silence of pre-teen me to the confident cyclist

crossing the land. I too am multitudes —
daughter, sister, mother, wife; student,
teacher, mentor, friend. Emerging

from this transient world into another
next new life, I'm the nervous girl
on her first day of school. Have I played

at being a vagabond? Or woman on a hero's
quest (with credit cards and cozy home,
a life to which I could always return)?

It was not by courage
but showing up, I cycled
a sixth of the earth.

The tide was up when I dipped a tire
into the cold of Casco Bay. Family
rejoined, my ride is done.

The world pours in.

Journey to Embarkation

A Way in the Wilderness
On Susan Richardson's cross-country trek while attending a workshop in Lake Louise, Alberta.

Ice encrusts your goggles
at twenty-five below.
Paths are sealed
in darkness, Lord!
There's no clear way to go.

And winter trails dim well
too fast as eventide
folds into night
with stars alone
providing light.

The world recedes as ways fall
dark and beauty
drains from mortal
sight, a silent prison
sealed in white.

While woods are lovely, dark and deep
when viewed from lodge
or well-groomed path,
sometime in life
will come a test

when woods turn into wilderness
when dark and deep
oppress the soul
when lovely turns
to creeping cold

your mind harks back to life before
spent safe beside the hearthstone
fire, which burns and brightens
even now in warmth
the lodge at Lake Louise.

You pause in awe of open sky
where holy visions
crystallize, as early
evening stars appear
with undreamed wonders

pressing near, beyond all words
but strangely clear
when set in stillness
white on white
so far from lodge at Lake Louise.

But ice encrusts your goggles,
it seeps inside
your soul, and time
compresses tightly
to frozen snowy hell

its icy heart, indifferent
to choices
and their toll.
So brave the cold,
embrace the pain

then take a step, and step again;
led by the arms of God to life
or to the arms of God to lie
matters not in wilderness –
resolve sustains

beyond despair if inner stillness
shares the grace
of snow white peaks
seen in the face
and placid depths of Lake Louise.

To the End of Haight
Golden Gate Park, San Francisco, California

It would be wrong, of course,
to hike up Haight in too new
tie dye, made in Haiti, hauled
to Georgia, bought off Hippies
costume rack, my own creation
(purple bled with golden high-
lights) gone to rags too long
ago.

I caught the Summer of Love
by the grace of my A.M. radio
while sweating construction
to finance my physics, and fantasized
Love-Ins were all I could muster
that innocent summer in North
Carolina.

Now here in Haight I haunt the places
free range hippies propagated
seeking *Authenticity* or failing
that, a clever tee to take back
home with burning words declaring
what it is we were, just what we
wanted life to hold, what never was
but still might be, in understated
irony.

From off the other side of Haight
persistent as the backed-up traffic
bold, phlegmatic yogi laughs
though not in mirth, but merely
practice. Blocks from fervor
gentry groom their comely rows
of reclaimed homes, each worth
more than all the flowers worn
by hippies in the Haight back in
the sixties.

With knowing smiles and narrowed
eyes, we've moved beyond the naïve
wise who fought for justice with those
flowers, summoned peace by sharing
song. Go gentle, people, after all
it's every generation's fate to re-enact
the Fall. Last call before we're ushered
out.

At the end of Haight the 'Golden Arches'
sits across from Whole Food Market
hard by parkland, pulsing, pulsing
tribal drums beat about the edge of awareness
from somewhere deep within the great long golden heart
that stretches out to the end of America
where sea fog gathers cleansing chill
close underground raw forces build
and the late day breeze drifts so gently
about my face, I cannot say which way
it blows.

Inner Sunset, Morning Rain
Japanese Tea Garden, San Francisco, California

My little girl leads me through her grown up world
of townhouses, trolleys, bodegas, cafes, and corner
stores. The smell of coffee cuts the soggy breeze.

Elsewhere the world churns. Fierce preachers poke
ancient wounds and politicians scratch the scabs.
Privilege feasts as Lazarus lies by padlocked gates.

Here, wizened men once interred in wartime camps
mingle with young mothers in yoga tights wielding
late-model strollers down the kinder sidewalks.

The streets of Inner Sunset are baptized in morning
rain. A small shop bears the sign—*Make loaves not
war.* We are far from the breaking madness, beyond

the contagion of hate. The implosion is put on hold.
In the face of chaos Mohammed went to the mountain
and Buddha withdrew. Even Jesus retreated. We enter

the garden and drift through a feather mist where sweet
plumes scent the heavy air. The city recedes. We trace
slow paths through flora that once graced Eden. White

blossoms litter the soft moss carpet beneath a baby cedar
grove. Gray rocks anchor grass islands in a raked sand
sea. We step to the trickle of cobblestone creeks and glide

past Koi ponds. A bronze Buddha, old as our country,
casts a placid spell on those who pause. The prophets
all returned. Mohammed spoke the Koran, Siddhartha

woke the Sangha, and Jesus preached the Kingdom.
We turn home together, bearing the grace of soft rain
in a parched land. Peace awaits in the folds of time.

Ladies of the Lake
Isle La Motte, Vermont

At Maya House
on Isle La Motte
two brides embrace

as loved ones watch
well-chosen words when
spoken under open sky

rise up in light
to join the song
of hermit thrush

in blissful flush
of summertime.
Soon siblings, strangers

sit as one, share
pasta, toasts and provolone
as Texas, Georgia, Quebecois

mingle with Missouri
tribes, their vegan plates
set side by side

with sausage balls
and biting flies, a wedding
feast for all alike.

Later in the failing light
beyond a summer sunset
far away from most places

rising over cold waters
a stone's throw
from rocky shores –

The ladies of the lake are one.

A Sunday Afternoon Island Dream
Isle La Motte, Vermont

Down at the Fisk farm,
four Vermont yankees
play the blues

to polite applause
beside the art barn
where the well

behaved sip unsweet
tea and lemonade
to wash down

deeply chocolate pie
on lawn chairs pulled
to patchy shade

as laid back bikers glide
slow roads that wind past
fields and cider

stands, which operate on
honor code, how goodness
goes in honest

lands, where in the deep late
afternoon a humble man
in holey jeans

strides up the road
with violin and soon
the early evening

still is gently filled
with Air on a G String
as maestro plays

Bach on the beach
with more passion
than skill, much

like most marriages,
which get by
on grace and guts

to kinder days,
like Isle La Motte,
its summertime

ice cider joy
distilled from bitter
winter nights.

A Friday Morning Devotional in Iglesia Evangelica Metodista
Los Angeles, Costa Rica

Listen. Echoes intermingle here
on the inside of a sweet instrument
projecting love with Latin flair,
where hearing is whole body and *fuego*
is a dance not confined to *Domingo*,
where decibels carry fevered joy deep
into small town nights.

Staccato hammer, hum of weld
that build and bind the world outside
are amplified within these walls
from tile floor to high eves and hiding
bats, they bounce back through,
they permeate the empty rows
of wooden pews.

The world intrudes on sacred space,
its hardened tones accentuate
the soft voice that weaves a world
of wise fools who bind the blessed
earth and sky with bold themes
and threads of hope

While high above, inside each pause
between rude strokes and spoken
words, bright notes proclaim to those
who hear what gospel truth wild
birds can sing.

And some hear more – a living spring
wells up from nothing pouring forth
between the notes with cleansing
uncontained by culture, unconstrained
by earnest creed.

So dance my love with fire and joy:
the emptiness, awash with angels, echoes
silent thoughts of God. Just listen, love
with body, soul and mind of faith
to hear its roar.

Jessica's Blessing
Mirador, Costa Rica

Trapped in the din of exuberance,
I shrink behind a stoic smile
as the children of Mirador
shake the sanctuary walls,
submerging senses,
drowning thought
in waves of chaos washing by,
composed of shouts
and soccer balls
giggling swirls of almond girls,
rice krispie squares
and lemonade,
the dreams they share of lives unfurled
beyond the world
of Mirador.

But can we ever comprehend
the calculus of blessings?
How karma comes so well
disguised. How butterflies
somewhere will sway, the wind
will shift another way,
and through the swirling stardust
currents, God speaks *Child*
to empire's fringe. How echoes
anchor minds that wander,
crack the armor, fill
the arms that ache to cradle,
fill the lives that ache
for more. And how the winds
of Mirador bestow
in trust a brown-eyed boy
to bind my soul a blessed
hour adrift on complicated
tides unbidden thoughts
impressed inside from child
or God I cannot say –

Are you among the modern magi,
those who wander far-off byways,
searching for a holy child
to bless with gifts then walk away
to one day join the jeering bands
in casting lots for what remains
when charity gets out of hand,
declares 'shalom' then works for change?

At the open church door, threshold
to the gleaming muddy world beyond,
a red-dress girl but five feet tall
lays down her youth, reclaims her child
and lifts the face of timid grace
to offer what she holds inside
her blessing, a beatitude —
Be happy, spoken word for me
from God or girl I cannot say.
Madonna child of fourteen years,
squares her back and turns away,
with watchful baby over shoulder
skips past puddles, rounds the corner,
treading lightly on the pathway
down her mud and gravel days.

The Night Music of San Rafael de Guatuso
San Rafael de Guatuso, Costa Rica

I wander dreams of dinosaurs
while dozing in a concrete cave
as freight trucks rumble
baritone scales
north into night.

Somewhere in darkness
drunks howl feigned joy
and small dogs strut
soprano outrage
from the safety of sofas.

Tremulations
stalk the hearts and haunt
the souls of those who walk
the night alone
in far lands.

But *far* is not a place you go to
far is something dark inside
a cave you wall against the terror
faced alone but not beyond
the love disguised as humble chance.

So who's to say the whippoorwill
who camps aside my weathered door
to chant his sad, hypnotic score
is not an angel sent by God
to guard the gap from black to gray

When somehow, dawn
birds sing back sleep
as light rains play
pianissimo
the green plains of Guatuso

Where fence posts sprout
leaves and roots, and dark nights
yield to sun drenched days
with black beans, bitter coffee
and sweet pineapple grace.

The Girl's Guava Tree
- and the good earth sustains
Mirador, Costa Rica

Beyond the gravel-pocked streets
lined with cinder-block shops

and child-packed homes
capped with corrugated tin

christened in the sweat of strangers
called from a far land

past the worn-out weed field
trampled by children to dusty flat

where rough tracks fork left
below fenced hills of cane and cattle

down, down the rutted path
to the rushing boulder stream

where a nimble girl parts barbed wire
and clambers up the guava tree

through distant light she smiles
and shares

Waiting for Advent in Istanbul
Istanbul, Turkey

Imprisoned in five-star comfort
on the edge of the Marmara Sea

I wake to the wail of the muezzin
calling the dark distance. Wrapped

in black sweats, wielding childhood
songs of hope, I work my way down

the cold shore where storm waves
disturb the well-groomed grounds.

Raw gusts probe bones as I wait
for dark to dissipate. December sun

rises red off an indistinct point
and slips behind the scud-black sky.

Egyptian Sunrise
Giza, Egypt, May 1982

Forgive me Amal, not knowing
your name, but it could not arise
in our improvised game,
that two-penny drama
played three decades past.

When we came to
Upper Kingdom elegance,
peers of a genteel breed
served thick bitter coffee
in tiny cups with a side
of sugar. Such a gracious land

of ruins and restaurants
fallucas on the Nile, sunsets
deep red with the dust of Sahara.
Of gentle dawns by slow waters
lapping riverbank reeds
where slave women once hid
baskets from Pharaoh's baleful
gaze. Pharaoh's eyes

still gaze unblinking
as he worships the gray
god Stability, secured
with burnt offerings —
the soul of a kingdom
locked down and torn
by the call of the dollar
and the call of the muezzin

in a mean land of dirt
and bribes, where swarms
of flies sip tears about
the soft brown eyes
of passive babes, born
to lives of hustling squalor.
Of grade school entrepreneurs

like you, Amal, rude son
of the Lower Kingdom,
your dark eyes discerning
where an impulse to kindness
might be mobilized to sustain

another day trolling tourists,
trading dignity for dollars
on dry sandstone bluffs
where must-see monuments
mark slow millennia
above the sprawl of Cairo.

You latched to us like desert flies
and even though we meant you
well, my bride and I could brook
no urge to mount tame camels
and make cheap postcards
to please people back home.
So we tipped you a bit to be
on your way, but *please*

and *no* are just weak
bids, and kind rejection
signals softness to sons
of Egypt, ever working
the tourist for just a bit
more. Dignity is a divide,
and no do-overs can bridge
culture and time. In the end

Amal, what is a pyramid
but a large pile of rock
burdened with too much
history? And *what is man
that Thou art mindful of him?*
Of you, Amal. Even you.

So if I could return
I would take you aside,
buy you bitter coffee,

the sweetest bread
and know a new soul,
both yours and my own.

I had not then read
Les Mis, or surely
would have recognized
le brun petit Gavroche,
so charming on the page,
but God help the mighty

when you turn your attention
from tourist to master
and meet the gaze of Pharaoh.
Did I see your son in Tahrir
Square, standing with the young
elite? Was that your girl
who turned a bronze cheek

to reclaim the honor
of Egypt? Dream big,
Amal, but know the score —
pathways to liberty
are negotiated on the backs
of tigers that care not

for your dreams.
They leave youthful
bodies, empty fathers
and hollow mothers
who nevermore live
whole. So be whole
Amal, bold child

of the human tribe.
May we meet once
more on the trembling
bridge that links time
and faith. Let me
shake your hand
this time around.

The Diminutive of Grace
Tianjin, China. For Xiang Wén Yàn (Gracie) and her father, Xiang Heng-Zhu

恩典

It can come anywhere,
which is why I travel,
why I make myself
stranger, bumbling

about the far ends,
seeking the epicenter
where subterranean
Grace probes thin places

and could even emerge
from the traffic of Tianjin
which, of course, it does
though we could not

know it just yet, caught
in the converging weave
of bikes and buses, trucks
and cars, each urgent

to shoot through now
to the next knot, and the next
in the wan afternoon light
of a jet-lagged Sunday.

恩典

Travel teaches hard truth –
Great Walls can be blocked
by blizzards, blogspot by
censors, blue sky by smog,

and old men mired in ideology
can meet in museums
by the mausoleum of Mao
to choose among themselves.

But Tao blows which way
it will and grace still flows
through whom it will.
Through tiny frames

born to mouse,
or to dragon, farm girls
from Hubei who pack fire
into forty kilos, carrying

a father's dream through
far cities, sustained
by songs of the Silver River
dividing celestial lovers

on dark nights far from
pavement. By small dogs
and bright days following
father through fields

feeding on stories, lessons
fit for weary souls — *When
days grow hard, remember
well the ones who hunger,*

*mountain children far
from school. And dear
Wén Yàn, do not forget
to feed your buffalo.*

恩典

I can still hear her song
soft in my ear, subtle
tones dancing gracefully
around my comprehension.

And I can still feel
her coarse silk warmth
resting on my right shoulder
in a tight bus barreling

through what time
we shared, what spirit
that smiles across culture
and binds the wounds of Babel.

恩典

This is why I travel, why
I cross the terminus
into tomorrow, to talk
in darkened halls the idiom

of equations, sharing
PowerPoints and polite
smiles, software suffused
with life-blood, coded bits

of mind, bequeathed.
But Gracie, did I never
lecture on the math
of absolute? A fraction

of the infinite
is infinite itself;
the diminutive
of Grace is grace.

Yangtze Blues
Three Gorges Dam Memorial Park, China

Far away, well east of Eden
virile rivers carved a valley
through the age of long ago.

Now stretching out in black earth flatness
cotton patch competes with paddy
tractor vies with buffalo
below the rolling orange groves
with fences lined in climbing jasmine
border rows of sycamore.

Here in the highlands of Hubei
I can hear its song
rising out of mist and mountain
gray home of gods now gone
refuge of wayfaring mystic and misfit
place where the wild torrent
courses through gorges
once upon some time ago.

But now the long river
languishes
flat and heavy
murky deepness drowns Three Gorges
sighs behind a concrete slab
controlled and still
until release.

To wander
ancient river plains
that birthed and nurtured
feudal lords

a brand new land
of grit and coal
of dusky skies
that smother cities

town and village
torn and pillaged
taken into concrete

borg till onward
into paradise
of tollway road

and high rise rows
in cities of ten million
souls, new centers

that were meant
to sparkle, broker
fortunes, beckon

dreams and draw
beleaguered masses
forward, soar

into the gray-brown
skyscape, lined
with cranes

and belching stacks
that stitch the land

and sky with smog
and seal the earth

beneath the load
of human progress.

East meets West
and ups the ante

heeds the siren
staggers forward

fading into midday haze.

And from the highlands of Hubei
so very far away from Eden
I can hear the good earth groaning
crushed beneath a billion souls
just seeking their century
salvation in wealth.

And so the modern world goes
as Gaia sighs and turns to stone
to wait upon a wiser age
when sages and keepers
will come once again.

Last November Sunset

The last November sunset
darkens to shadows
on the stubble horizon

when off a distant ridge, December
wind clears warmth
from a once promising day

and the heart of a hundred billion
suns smears cold
light across velvet silence.

A spare beauty bears the hint
of primal heat
through widening gulfs

to fallow souls rooted in lost time
waiting for winter
to spring new seed from sweet decline.

To Go to Patagonia
January ruminations on a Sunday Times travel section

Some truths hover
just past the point of perception
and pass into knowing
gradual as gray dawn

grows from blue-black nights
to gentle winter days in Georgia
singing frost and white camellia,
silver age and pale regret:

*You'll never go to Patagonia
never trek the tortured plain
to breathe the bracing air of Andes
blowing off the icy seas.*

*You'll never see auroras dance
unless by chance coronas leap
and sear the Southern sky with fire
an hour before your time of sleep.*

*You'll go no more to Mykenos
nevermore return to youth
to stride the sands of Paradise
while clothed in fresh Aegean air.*

Some truths lie
harmless as hibernating vipers
that wake on warm days
to feed on minds that give them life.

But winter afternoons can glow
as silver yields to tones of gold
and old camellias burst in color –
so it is with elder souls

who step beyond belief and doubt,
and freed at last of empty strife
embrace the wondrous, fallen world
which harbors grace within the shadows.

From this veil I would chase truths
past the far end of perception
where they flit, unformed
above a lonely Patagonia

where somehow, surely
amidst the sun-drenched daydreams of God
my doppelgänger draws near
the Torres del Paine.

Afternoon Joe

You smile into a steaming cup
in search of grounds and gracious lines
to share with he in painter's cap
who holds up signs by traffic stops
where hand-drawn letters spell the barter,
work for food, but what he offers:
one more try for wary drivers —
multiply the fish and loaves
within the gap from red to green.
But eyes averted never see
the narrow Galilean path
that stretches off another way
beyond the light that guides the flow
from bank to drugs to Chick-fil-A
and on to homes to huddle nights
encased in husks of wood and cheer,
which fortify a life's veneer
in hoarded warmth

                        but those like Joe
spend hours in the public square
and nurse their warmth from cardboard
cups – a Big Joe buys an afternoon
of comfort on a well-used couch
amidst assorted Macs and pads
and textbooks cracked by pert coeds
in gym shorts, flip-flops, painted toes
and funky guys in baggy clothes,
by nursing interns sporting scrubs
and midlife strivers buttoned up,
a young instructor talking math
by Chinese couples lugging packs,
a working mother, child in tow —
they come and go and barely note
an old man whiling time alone
and gentle souls at rest, like Joe

who on a warm midafternoon
could tell you how to weather cold
through cruel nights that numb the soul,
when howling Arctic winter lows
pile snow on sagging canvas homes,
the weak won't make the morning call
in trembling walls of flesh and fabric;
battered down, resigned to die,
the voice of God

    commands we rise
    and manufacture right
    on ice, from slush
    a snowman shrine to life
    submerging fear
    in warmth of play
    through bitter night
    to brittle day

        and yes I too
I mean to say have felt my heart so
strangely warmed behind my silent
public smile my words are snowmen
guarding night and creeping numbness
in my life, but first retreat to resupply
the cardboard warmth to ease
the ties of mid-day neighbors, even
Joe who, unobtrusive, slipped away
somewhere along the ancient path
to find a home beneath the sky.

Watching After August Rains

Come the season of crow and cicada
in the stasis of late summer
when old dogs and aging men
laze about their porches, waiting

perhaps to watch a raucous squad
maneuver through the understory
working the wide angles
ever closer, closing in

to stage a raid on take home tins
containing bits of doggie kibble
left from last night's feeding.
Let them have it all, I whisper

staring down long moments
on a languid frame of fur and bones
to spot a shallow tell-tale breath.
Sleep, not death, not yet, not yet.

Good 'Ole Bowser, last of litter
just another Georgia black dog
brought in from the woods.
Seen fifteen summers, asks so little —

tummy rubs and idle scritches,
snuffle walks around the back,
some kitchen scraps atop his kibble.
Let black birds have what he won't eat.

We grow complacent waiting, waiting.
Far away the world lurches,
the young return to learning,
the busy go their scripted way.

You who strive and chase the wind
bursting with certain conviction,
would you pause and sit a while
to watch an August day with me?

For I have seen sixty-five summers
that once seemed centuries
in a lifetime of forever
but from the distance of back decks

the days may drag
but years by God
are short. They lead
to spent seasons

tired dogs, and yearnings
which have no name
borne on a fresh westerly
clearing out the August rain.

From the Deck of the New Horizons

I have been here before, swept
to the stars by an artist's rendition
bound in my childhood Book
of Knowledge. Lost in the pages

on Pluto, I stood on a cracked
and frozen plain where Sol is
but the brightest star whose light
is hours old. From eternal

twilight I turned my back
to the sun-bathed Earth, seared
by the ancient, wandering call,
set off to inhabit infinity.

-

On a farther end of forever
I find myself as in a dream
sailing shotgun on a spacecraft
the size of a grand piano
at the climax of a nine-year fling
approaching the double-dwarf
planetoid world which waltzes
with Charon face to face
on a multi-century solar swing
in two/three time with Neptune.

-

I fly by the moons of Hydra and Styx
the realm of Kerberos and Nix

dodging the darkened pole of Charon
covered with cryo-geyser debris

I shoot past the methane plains of Pluto
over the frozen Sputnik Planum

above the Virgil Fossa Canyon
land where ice volcanos flow.

I see a strangely familiar world —
a touch of haze in the light blue sky

as warm days climb to fifty-three Kelvin
across the fields of crystallized nitrogen

mountains of ice as high as the Rockies
dusted with hydrocarbon snow.
-

I have been here before, swept
aloft to far-off worlds. Now
I gaze behind to a sun-bathed
youth lost in a dream that could

never come close to riding
the deck of the New Horizons
Pluto in the rear-view mirror
universe ahead.

Light Bodies

Forged from Light
and Will to Be
condensing bits
of information

spare abstractions
bare equations birthed
in time to earthen bodies
word and dust

made humankind
where thoughts careen
through three pound prisons
fired by feelings

primal scream
to tribal voodoo,
nursery rhyme
to alleluia.

A thousand tongues sing broken
rhyme, ten thousand voices vie
for time in neural networks
born to die, yet something watches

deep inside —
freedom is a mirrored maze
with no path back
and branches split forever forward

built atop the tangled byways
burrowed deep within the psyche
trapped by musty cells inside
the catacombs of joy and tears.

But out beyond all self-reflection
past the chain of explanation
unconstrained by mere causation
life abundant whispers, dear

you are your light body
the woken one
serene as Siddhartha
sharing his smile

the soul of Yeshua
encircled by sinners
with stones in hand
and softening hearts.

Yours is the earth of Adam
the wind of Lao Tzu
the fire of Elijah, yours
the still waters.

Let go the deathly grip on grace
and loose the light body —
your own true face awaits
the joining.

Lessons for the Fallen

When you find your life, fallen;
when you inhabit the gap,
the no longer but not yet,
the neither-nor:

Then linger, friend;
let the soft day suffice;
do not rush the soon to be,
do not claw back the packaged past.

When you find yourself caught
in-between, your stance astride
both deck and dinghy, rope
untethered, weather rising:

Do not stand tall and grasp the wind;
forego, my friend, the stately pose
but sink your soul below the storm
and praise the passing of the waves.

When you find your soul, riven;
when truths refuse to reconcile;
when torn between two warring armies
dug in trenches, steel points gleaming:

Then light your last candle;
make your way to no-man's land
beyond the barbed wire and bayonet,
and sing your hymn on holy ground.

The Second Soul of November

    Call me Aquarius
unlike Ishmael, set to sea
by soul's November
damp and drizzle
cold November
grim about the mouth
November
chased into the arms of Ahab
ever striving, ever driving
raging to the fading light
in endless existential angst
aspiring to redeeming greatness
spurning fear and hope alike
embracing *Übermensch* inside

    which elevates
    contentious ways
    defines the dark
    in dismal days
    descends again
    the well of cold
    which holds the dread
    November soul

Well goodness gracious that
November, bless its existential
heart, so *Sturm und Drang*, so
not my drama. Mine the mellow
Southern season mixing mild
with bracing days, when
woodlands open up and welcome
winter's heart of tan and brown.
There's peace in piercing shafts
of sunlight slowly warming forest
floor where solemn anoles fade
in silence, green to tan in golden
sun. There's grace in shy suburban
does when flushed from front yard

flower gardens, gracile statues
snapped to life and soaring lightly
through the early evening shadows
cast by rising Hunter's Moon.
November's second soul is sweetness
wrapped in dwindling light and life,
a treasure passed unrecognized
by those who set themselves
to sea

    immersed
    and haunted
    ever onward
    driven, seeking
    never finding
    ever scanning
    endless oceans
    screaming
    squid-breath
    over here, ya
    wanna 'nother
    piece a' me?

Though some still think to call
it glory – deeply woven hero
story – manning up is in our guts,
in coded genes we cannot break,
but fallen human spirit grows
new harmonies will soon take hold
November's grace will seep inside
and ground the mind of greatness yet.

    So never mind
    the date precisely
    when my fate shall
    breach beside me,
    when the white whale
    comes for me, I'll draw
    upon that second soul
    to harness what I have

in store to bless the beast
that looms before me,
bless the beast that lurks
inside, to look with love
on ice cold eyes, to look
my last on open skies,
to fill my lungs with light
and dive.

Journey to Embarkation
Daejeon, South Korea

Midnight rains have stopped for now
and veils of mist envelop trees. Soft
textures of darkness hover beyond
    the pale reach of streetlight
that bathes the last bus stop
        out of Daejeon.

Late night truths come veiled in signs.
A white dog emerges from shadow,
makes his mark then passes on
    and leaves me emptied
on the path of pilgrim now
        at peace with night.

Though dawn lies distant, far beyond
my closed horizons bright midmorning
showers light, I must have faith
    for here I am, wayfaring
stranger, watching forms
        in drifts of fog.

Too soon the rains will return
and the lullaby tap of wipers
will soothe intermittent sleep
    through the last
empty hours of night
        in a far country,

And my bus will plow steady
to causeway's end
beyond the mudflats
    where sea and sky
merge, gray and indistinct
        at Incheon.

My brothers, we are bodies
becoming spirit, forever drifting
mid-transit. We are always
    awaiting embarkation.
We have always already
        arrived.

Postlude

A Remembrance of Terminals Past
Austin-Bergstrom International Airport, Austin, Texas

If I had paid the fifty-dollar fee
for an early flight out of Austin
I would not have heard Willie sing

a laconic Christmas soundtrack
as I drift through torpor, bored
yet blessed by sunny Gate 6.

I watch a flight leave for Atlanta.
The tarmac gleams. Giant craft
snuggle favored gates like rows

of piglets on a sideways sow.
Slumped in a rigid airport chair,
I sink within my hooded cloak,

comfortable as an arthritic cat.
Riding the scent of sweet buns
and mocha, I enter the timeless

travel haze. The world passes with
apparent purpose. A flight arrives.
Someone sprints. I glimpse again

my younger self striding corridors
of airports. Was it in a hall at SFO
(or a dream of the Gombe jungle)

when I breezed past an elderly
Jane Goodall without a sideways
glance? Was I stuck at Xiamen

(or was it Fuzhou) when my watcher
taught me tai chi? Another flight rolls
away from my gate and I live again

the afternoon waiting in an Aswan
lounge (ticket untaken and boarding
pass bumped) watching tour groups

return to Cairo. A small fan stirred
stale air. My schedule wilted. Gate
agents drank sweet tea, unconcerned:

I would leave that day, *inshallah*,
make my hotel before midnight,
and be home again soon enough.

I'll be home again soon enough.

Acknowledgments

I gratefully acknowledge the thriving Athens poetry community, which has nurtured my writing for the past seven years. The Athens Word of Mouth community, founded by Aralee Strange, has provided a monthly public forum for spoken word poetry.

The weekly Donderos' workshop has provided a setting for sharing and critiquing written poems. My colleagues include Gene Bianchi, Mark Bromberg, Greg DeRocher, Sam Lane, Sharon McCoy, David Noah, and David Oates.

Michelle Castleberry hosted monthly Firemouth Salon workshops, providing prompts, inspiration, food, and fellowship.

www.ingramcontent.com/pod-product-compliance
Lightning Source LLC
Chambersburg PA
CBHW052101110526
44591CB00013B/2308